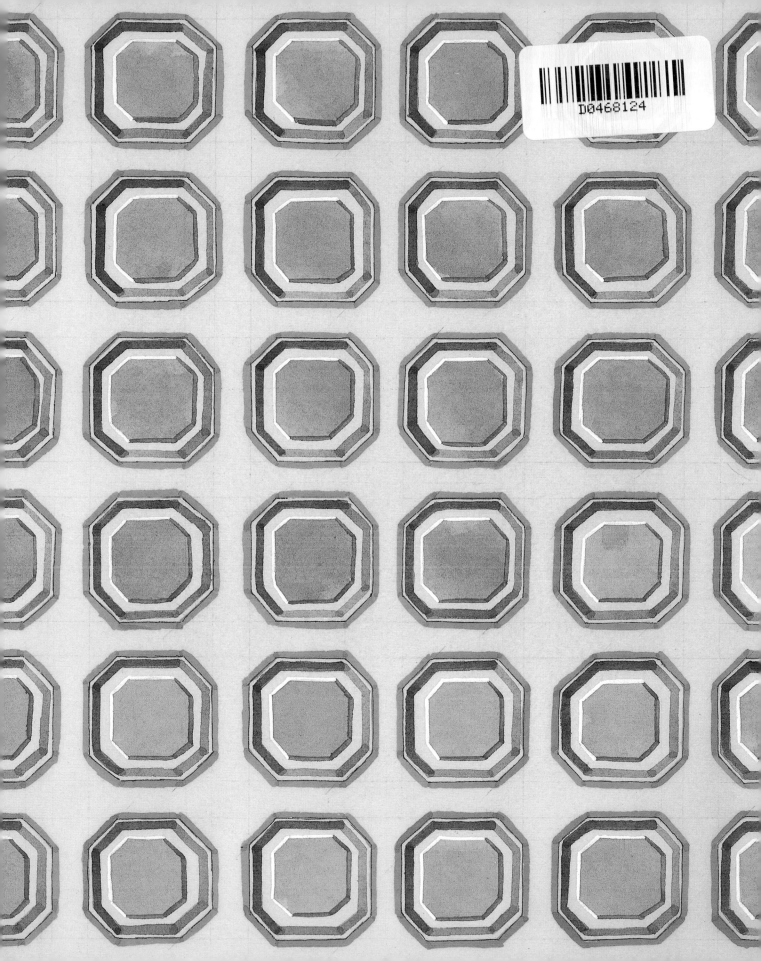

by Harriet Berg Schwartz

BACKSTAGE WITH CLAWDIO

illustrated by David Catrow

ALFRED A. KNOPF, PUBLISHER
New York

The illustrator would like to extend special thanks
to Robyn Howard of Ballet Met for her kind assistance.

THIS IS A BORZOI BOOK PUBLISHED BY ALFRED A. KNOPF, INC.

Text copyright © 1993 by Harriet Berg Schwartz
Illustrations copyright © 1993 by David J. Catrow

All rights reserved under International and Pan-American Copyright Conventions.
Published in the United States by Alfred A. Knopf, Inc., New York, and
simultaneously in Canada by Random House of Canada Limited, Toronto.
Distributed by Random House, Inc., New York. Book design by Edward Miller.

Library of Congress Cataloging-in-Publication Data

Schwartz, Harriet Berg. Backstage with Clawdio
/ by Harriet Berg Schwartz ; illustrations by David J. Catrow.
p. cm.
Summary: Clawdio the theater cat describes how he keeps everything running
smoothly backstage during a production of *Peter Pan*. ISBN 0-679-81763-8 (trade)
— ISBN 0-679-91763-2 (lib. bdg.) [1. Theater—Fiction. 2. Cats—Fiction.]
I. Catrow, David, ill. II. Title. PZ7.S40765Bac 1993 [E]—dc20 92-21683

Manufactured in the United States of America
2 4 6 8 0 9 7 5 3 1

To David
—H. B. S.

To Donna, our lifeguard
—D. C.

E very good theater has a cat. My name is Clawdio, and I am a theater cat. My mother, Catisha, and my father, Curtains, both theater cats until their recent retirement, taught me everything I know.

I do my job of stage manager's assistant well, and I always have a warm, dry place to sleep, good food to eat, and the respect of my fellow toilers on the boards.

For the past few months a hit revival of a play called *Peter Pan* has been running. It's about a boy who never grows up, and there are eight shows a week: Wednesday and Saturday matinees and every night except Sunday.

An hour before each performance, I stand at the backstage entrance with Joe the doorman and greet the actors.

Sometimes a fan who wants an autograph will try to sneak past, but I take care of that.

"Mmmeeeoooowww!"
I must be careful not to offend. Fans are the lifeblood of us theater professionals.

Madge Millikin, who plays Mrs. Darling,
the mother, waits for me at the stage door.

I escort her through the darkness to her dressing room,
over thick electric cables used for lighting and sound equipment,

around the Darlings' furniture, past Captain Hook's deck,
and behind the backdrop of Neverland.

Soon all the actors are in their dressing rooms, putting on costumes and makeup. They dress like their characters, exaggerating their eyes, lips, and cheeks with rouge and face pencils so they can be seen by the audience sitting far away.

But the actor playing Nana, the nurse, doesn't wear makeup. Nana is a big Newfoundland dog who must make beds, run bathwater, and carry an umbrella. Can you imagine any dog smart enough? Of course, it's really a human in a costume, crawling around.

Sitting on Captain Hook's dressing table, I too take a few moments to spruce up. Some may call this vanity, but I believe we theater folk must always look our best. Our public expects it.

Next it's time to calm the actors. Jennifer Haskell, who plays Peter, suffered a severe attack of stage fright on opening night. With a full house—every seat taken— Jenny sat shivering backstage, afraid to go on!

I hopped into her lap. "RRRrrr, RRRrrr," I said.

"*You* don't have stage fright, do you, Clawdio?" What a
question! With my tradition, inheritance, background? As
she stroked me and I purred, I felt her relax. Need I
explain that Jenny went on to rave reviews? Or that now
she's a Broadway star? Like all true greats, Jennifer Haskell
remembers who set her feet on that first rung of the ladder
to stardom. She remembers *me*. Every day she brings me
a tasty bit of steak or Nova Scotia salmon.

Peter Pan offers a true challenge to the busy theater cat
because there is so much stage machinery lying about.
Some is used to make Peter, Wendy, and her brothers fly

from the nursery to Neverland. The actors are attached
to very strong wires, which, when the right buttons are
pushed, hoist them up, up, up into the air!

A peculiar thing happened during a dress rehearsal.

"Yikes!" Wendy cried as she went flying up in the air, instead of climbing into bed.

"What's going on around here!" screamed Sherwood Nottingham, the director.

"Don't yell at me, Boss!" Johnny, a stagehand, shouted back. "It was Clawdio underfoot again. Scat!"

This is how a theater cat can become unemployed. Of course, my backstage crew knew that the play could never go on without me, so my job was safe.

A half hour before curtain time, Mr. Beecham, the stage manager, says, "Hop to it, Clawdio!" and rings the warning bell. Off I go, padding around to all the dressing rooms.

"Meeoow!" Half hour till curtain, Madge. "Meeoow!" Half hour, Jenny. I'll dash around again at the fifteen-minute bell, and again at five minutes before show time.

Then I move on to the front of the theater. Have the street doors been unlocked? Are there stacks of programs for tonight's performance? Are the ushers at their stations? Backstage again, I peep from behind the curtain to watch the audience take their seats.

I look around. Is the scenery in the right place? Are the
props ready and where they belong? Is the bed on its marks?
Is the tablecloth straight? Because the stage is still
dark, my sharp eyes are needed.

When I rub against Mr. Beecham's leg, he knows
it's time to call "Places, everyone!"

The houselights dim, and the stage lights come up. The curtain rises. The great moment is upon us—the play begins!

I sit absolutely still, watching and listening. Suddenly, everything is true. Peter and the children can fly. The nurse is a Newfoundland dog.

Captain Hook falls overboard into the jaws of a crocodile. The flapping red and yellow rags are a hot fire. Peter loves Wendy. Because we all believe these things together — all of us, the actors and the audience and the backstage crew — all of us together, at the same time in the same place, the world on the stage becomes the only real world.

When the play is over, the curtain falls. It goes up again while the audience claps and the actors take their bows. The curtain comes down again and stays down. The strong stage lights are turned off.

The audience leaves the theater, and the actors head backstage to take off their costumes and remove their makeup. The stagehands set up the scenery for the beginning of the play for tomorrow's performance.

"Good night, Joe. Good night, Clawdio." Mother is really Madge Millikin again. Peter Pan is really shy Jennifer Haskell. Nana the Newfoundland dog hangs limply on the costume rack. The magic world of the stage has disappeared until tomorrow.

I roam around backstage one final time. It is dark now, except for the single work light that burns all night on the stage. Has everyone gone? The stage fireplace is cold, the stage bed too hard to sleep on. I sniff at the greasepaint. It smells better than catnip to a theater cat.

At last, I curl up on a velvet cushion made from an old theater seat and doze until it is time for work again.

GLOSSARY

Autograph
A signature. Some fans collect autographs of stars.

Backdrop
A painted curtain hung at the back of the stage, showing the background of the scene.

Backstage
The parts of the theater the audience never sees, behind and to the sides of the stage.

Boards
The stage. The earliest stages were on the back ends of carts made of wooden boards. "Toilers on the boards" are people who work in the theater.

Broadway
A street in New York City whose name has been given to the theater district there, the center of theater in the United States.

Crew
All the people (except the actors, writers, and producers) who work together to put on a play.

Director
The person who supervises all the elements of the play and tells everyone what to do.

Fan
Short for "fanatic." A great admirer of a famous person or activity.

Greasepaint
A makeup base of colored ointment that is worn under face powder. It comes in every shade from white to black.

House
The theater, excluding the stage and backstage areas. A "full house" means that all the seats are taken. The "houselights" are the lights in the audience's part of the theater. The "front of the house" is the auditorium and lobby.

Marks
Painted lines or dots on the stage showing where scenery should be placed and where actors should stand.

Matinee
A performance given in the daytime, usually the afternoon.

Places
Where the actors are supposed to be when the play begins.

Program
A booklet or printed sheet that gives the title of the play and the names of the author, the actors, and all the other people who worked to put on the play.

Props
Short for "properties." Things the actors actually pick up and use on the stage, like a book or a telephone.

Rehearsal
A practice performance of the play before acting it in front of an audience. The "dress rehearsal" is the final practice, when the play is performed just as it will be for the audience.

Revival
A new production of an old play that may not have been performed for some time.

Run
The number of days, weeks, months, or years that a play is performed continuously. A play is "running" when it is being performed day after day. The "running time" is the length of time it takes to perform the play from beginning to end.

Stage Door
The back door of the theater.

Stage Fright
Fear of going onto a stage and acting in front of an audience.

Stage Manager
The overall supervisor of the crew and actors. Second in command to the director.

Stagehand
Someone who sets up and moves the scenery and props.

Star
A performer who is famous enough to have his or her name written above the name of the play on the program and in front of the theater. However, the term is often used only to mean a very well known actor.

Usher
Someone who shows the members of the audience to their seats.